CONTENTS

GW00360538

GENERAL LEARNING OBJECTIVES OF THIS UNIT

This Open Learning Unit will supply you with the core information you need to answer examination questions or to write an essay on adolescence, adulthood and senescence. It will take you 3 or 4 hours to work through, though if you attempt all the suggested activities it might well take longer.

By the end of this Unit you should understand:

▷ the social, cultural and individual factors affecting the human journey through life;

▷ the effects of physical and psychological change on human beings as they grow older;

▷ the influences of family, peer group and employment, and the effects of particular life events such as marriage, parenting, divorce, loss and bereavement, unemployment and retirement.

Introduction

Adolescence, adulthood and ageing have attracted a great deal of interest from psychologists this century. But their explanations for what exactly happens during this period differ. Some psychologists focus on the importance of the inner life of the individual. Other psychologists prefer to emphasize the shaping role of the environment upon individuals, citing not just the family but also peers and experience in the community as highly important influences. A third school of thought stresses the importance of genetic inheritance, personal temperament, and previous intellectual experience. A fourth school focuses upon every different influence affecting the individual at any one time, both internally and externally from the general environment.

All these approaches include a certain amount of overlap with each other, and all have something to offer the understanding of adolescence, adulthood and ageing. Let's look at each one in more detail.

The psychoanalytic approach

Psychoanalysts see the development and successful management of sexual feeling as a most important factor in understanding human beings. Erik Erikson (1968), working from his own psychoanalytic perspective, focused on how adolescents often break with established family patterns and look for a new sense of identity. Until they feel confident in this new identity, adolescents are thought to experience an unsettling time of storm and stress while perpetually trying to answer the question: 'Who am I?' Parents may also sometimes behave insensitively during this

1

period, some of them possibly jealous of their adolescent's growing sexuality at a time when they may be starting to feel their age themselves. How well these early crises are resolved will have an important effect upon future development in adulthood.

The sociological approach

Sociologists tend to stress the contradictory social demands made upon individuals in Western societies. While most people have firm expectations about what sort of behaviour to expect from children and adults, attitudes to adolescence are often more confused. A parent or teacher may still treat an adolescent as a child, while a friend may expect them to be more grown-up. Adolescents will also be exposed to many contrasting influences, from those held by their own peer group to different political, religious or social ideas they hear about and encounter elsewhere. Instead of following their parents' beliefs as before, adolescents now often make up their own minds for themselves. The effort needed in trying to resolve these conflicting pressures is thought to make adolescence a potentially difficult time, once again having an important effect upon future adult development. This view was best put forward over 60 years ago by Ruth Benedict (1934).

The cognitive approach

A third perspective stresses the importance of the intellectual development taking place at the time of puberty and beyond, thereby allowing the individual to address more complex intellectual issues. According to Piaget's theory (see the companion unit, *Cognitive and Language Development*, by Peter Lloyd) at around the age of eleven children become capable of abstract thinking. This new ability helps them to tackle topics like the algebra taught in the early years of secondary school, or the complexities raised by philosophy and religion. Adolescence therefore can also be characterized by the questioning that arises when individuals use their new ability to look more critically at their own values as well as those held by their parents and by society at large. Maintaining confidence in one's right and ability to ask questions and then to assess the answers received in a satisfactory manner is another important attribute of personal confidence during the rest of adulthood.

The lifespan approach

The belief here is that personal development involves a highly complex interaction of many different influences. **Cognitive** factors, the influence of the family and an individual's own genetic make-up and temperament must be balanced against influences arising from the geographical, social and political setting in which they live. Different social settings lead to different personal experiences. The particular character of an individual will also have an important bearing in the way they set about shaping their own development. Unlike psychoanalytic theories of personal development, lifespan developmental psychology declines to make rules about individual experience. Instead, it emphasizes the importance of the way each individual reacts within what may often be very different social worlds. For further discussion on the lifespan approach, see the companion unit *Aspects of Human Development* by Charlie Lewis.

Summary

Psychoanalytic and sociological theories successfully explain the behaviour of some individuals. Yet where adolescence in particular is concerned, both fail to account for the many individuals who remained friendly with their parents and who did not suffer any particular 'storm and stress' or crisis of identity. Coleman and Hendry (1990) prefer the lifespan model for understanding adolescence, but add their own 'focal' theory. This states that while different important issues generally come into focus at different times during adolescence, those individuals who experience a number of problems or major life changes all at once are going to be at greater risk. To understand this theory better, look at Figure 1.

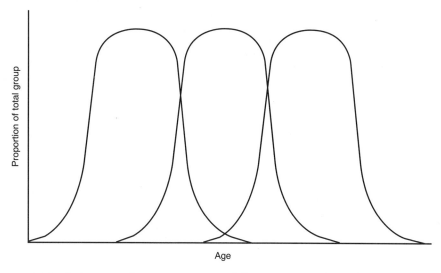

FIGURE 1. *Focal theory. Each curve represents a different issue or relationship.* From Coleman and Hendry (1990)

Each curve in Figure 1 represents a different issue or relationship during adolescence. Reading from left to right, let's suppose they represent conflict with parents, fear of rejection from the peer group, and anxiety about heterosexual relationships. Looking at Coleman and Hendry's model, you can deduce that adolescents around the top of the first curve may be experiencing conflict with their parents but have yet to fear rejection from their own peer group. When the adolescent has grown older (towards the end of the first curve), they may by now be experiencing both problems. And those older still and now at the very bottom of the first curve may, for a short time in their lives, be experiencing all three problems at once.

Coleman and Hendry do not claim that conflict with parents, fear of rejection by the peer group and anxiety over heterosexual relationships necessarily follow each other in a time sequence. Each of the curves on this model could stand for a different issue or relationship affecting adolescents. What the model does suggest is that during adolescence one major problem may sometimes have to be tackled before another, older problem has been resolved. At these times, adolescents may be more stressed than at other moments when one problem has more or less been sorted out, leaving them free to tackle the next one.

Individual **temperament** will also play a large part: while a fiery adolescent may quarrel with a parent, a teacher and a friend all in one day, more placid individuals may be able to make life easier for themselves by having the right temperament to live with more than one problem at a time.

Rather than necessarily choosing between these different interpretations of personal development, most psychologists will select what they see as the best contributions from each approach. It obviously matters what individuals bring with them into the world by way of inheritance and temperament. What happens next, in terms of local environment and type of school can also be of great significance. How anyone gets on with their parents when young can also make a large difference to their lives. Disentangling the importance of all these different influences coming to bear upon one individual is always going to be a difficult task, with no promise of any final agreement between different experts. But to be in a position to understand how psychologists come to their sometimes differing conclusions, it is necessary first to discover how much is known about different periods of personal growth, starting with adolescence. What exactly does the word mean?

SAQ 1

Which of the different theories of adolescence point to the importance of the environment: psychoanalytic, sociological, cognitive or lifespan?

1 Adolescence

KEY AIMS: By the end of Part 1 you will be able to:
- ▷ *define adolescence*
- ▷ *describe the most important factors affecting adolescents*
- ▷ *reject some of the myths about 'typical' adolescent behaviour.*

What is adolescence?

Adolescence is the period of life between childhood and adulthood. In some traditional societies, its beginning is marked by a particular ceremony held at a certain age or at a fixed time in the year. But in the Western world, no one knows for sure when it actually starts or finishes. The word means 'growing up', but who can say when this process begins or stops?

We talk about a mature child as having an old head on young shoulders, and an adult as sometimes enjoying a second childhood. What do you think are the principal differences between children and adults?

The period of growth spurt and sexual development known as **puberty** accompanies adolescence. Puberty is a physical process which develops in orderly, unmistakable stages. Adolescence is a period of time during which an individual gradually changes from child to adult; it may start with puberty, but not necessarily. Some girls start **menstruating** as early as ten, yet one hardly thinks of adolescents as primary school pupils. Boys usually start puberty after girls, sometimes as late as 14 or 15, but this does not mean they continue to remain children until puberty finally arrives.

SAQ
2

What is the difference between adolescence and puberty?

Some adolescents may appear quite adult while others still look like children. They do not always know whether they want to be treated as children or as near-adults, and society itself provides mixed messages. For example, in Britain you can marry at 16 with parental consent, but you are not allowed to drive till 17 and you cannot vote, watch certain films or buy alcohol until you are 18. No wonder some adolescents are confused!

Some believe that adolescence finishes at the end of full-time education, when young people are expected to start supporting themselves. But 16-year-old school-leavers can hardly be considered to be adults; only by 18 will they have full grown-up status in law, and it still might take some time for older adults to start treating them as equals. Further education students are financially dependent on their parents up to 21 or beyond, although their thinking processes may become far more adult during this time. One can therefore only approximately guess when adolescence finishes, based on each individual concerned and what particular stages they seem to have started, experienced or finally left behind.

So how shall we define adolescence? The safest answer is: 'An extended period when a number of important physical, intellectual, social and emotional changes take place.' Family and society mark these changes by reacting differently to the individual concerned, often expecting more from them.

But experience of so many changes over a few years does not necessarily cause inevitable difficulties, as was once thought. Evidence suggests that each person's journey through adolescence is an individual matter. To understand why, we must look in more detail at the particular emotional, cultural and social circumstances of each individual and how these affect their experience of the changes which occur during adolescence. Studying the biology of adolescence is never going to be enough to provide explanations of behaviour. Even more important is how each individual reacts to the changes taking place within them, and how society in turn then reacts to the adolescent either as an individual or as part of a group.

What rights should a 15-year-old be granted? Tick the box you most agree with. Count up the points indicated in the circles you have ticked to see how strict you think parents should be.

1. *Bedtime.* Fixed time during school. ① Some negotiation. ② Any time. ③

2. *Personal appearance.* Strict rules. ① A few rules. ② Anything goes. ③

3. *Own income.* Limited pocket money. ① A few larger sums, for example dress allowance. ② As much money as you want. ③

4. *Independence (telling parents where you are and what you will be doing).* Should always say. ① Should sometimes say. ② Total freedom to come and go as you please. ③

5. *Homework.* Strict parental supervision. ① Some parental supervision. ② No parental supervision. ③

6. *Sexual relationships with others.* Strict parental control. ① Some parental control. ② No parental control. ③

6 points = strict parenting
12 points = moderate parenting
18 points = permissive parenting

Now score the test in the way you think your parents would answer it.
How does your own score compare with what you imagine theirs would be? Are there any major disagreements? Have these sometimes led to arguments?

Physical changes

The growth spurt for boys means an increase in height and in shoulder breadth and muscle. Girls also grow in height and weight, usually starting around the age of ten-and-a-half, or an average two years earlier than boys. Development in motor and athletic skills may lead to better performance in skilled work or on the sports field. Both boys and girls develop sexually during this time.

Growth in height, strength and sexual attractiveness is usually welcomed by both sexes. Research over the past 20 years has suggested that the timing of these physical changes is important and may be crucial in influencing the individual's adjustment to early adolescence. Boys who mature early tend to be more popular and socially relaxed, possibly as a result of greater strength which is often put to good effect in sports. But boys who mature late sometimes become self-conscious about their small stature. Male adolescents who are overweight may also worry about their size and occasional clumsiness.

Unlike boys, girls may not always welcome early physical maturation. Some are troubled by the fact that they tend to be heavier than average, since female adolescents often experience an increase in hip width and an accumulation of fat as they stop growing taller. This concern about body image can be made worse by teasing from others; it is also not helped by an over-emphasis in the media upon the importance of looking slim. Unlike boys, girls who are most satisfied with their bodies tend to be underweight, which explains why so many adolescent girls experiment with dieting, usually ineffectively (Attie and Brooks-Gunn, 1989).

Figure 2 shows the different effects of the timing of puberty on males and females. For boys, the earlier the onset of puberty the more positive is the change in their confidence and self-esteem. For girls, the timing is best if not 'too early' (i.e. before their friends) or 'too late' (i.e. after everyone else).

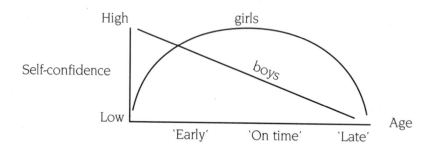

FIGURE 2. *The relationship between self-confidence and the timing of puberty in males and females.*

SOMETHING TO TRY
Look at the first ten advertisements featuring pictures of female models in a magazine aimed at younger female readers. Are the models extra slim, normal or overweight? How many references to dieting can you see? Now look at Roget's Thesaurus. *How many different mocking words can you find to describe someone who is 'fat' compared with someone who is 'thin'? What does this suggest about the pressure upon adolescents about their body weight?*

With the growth of sexual feeling, adolescents are frequently concerned about how attractive they are to the opposite sex. Hormonal changes can stimulate the **sebaceous** glands to produce acne at this age, which can prove embarrassing. Adolescents who are seen as attractive have an easier time, since they are more likely to enjoy positive reactions from others. Yet most adolescents get by, given sufficient support from family and friends. Only a few become seriously depressed because of anxiety about their physical appearance.

The family's attitudes to physical changes and sexuality has an important bearing on how adolescents feel about their own physical development. In some parts of the world, a girl's first menstrual period is greeted by a family party and general rejoicing. Greater privacy is the norm in the Western world. This may be a problem if such privacy also promotes feelings of shame and disgust over what is normal and desirable development. But attitudes are changing and only a minority of girls are still likely to view **menstruation** as the 'curse'.

SAQ
3

Is it true that the dramatic bodily changes occurring over a short period of time almost always cause some anxiety among adolescents?

Intellectual changes

Most adolescents develop a new capacity for abstract thought; they can now think more logically. They are capable of considering and assessing a wide variety of statements and ideas, since they are able to go beyond the actual or concrete in their thinking, and understand also the possible and the theoretical.

For example, take the following statement: 'Mary was a bad Queen of England because she ordered that Protestant martyrs be burned at the stake'. Younger children would immediately accept that anyone who ever ordered death in this manner must be bad. Adolescent pupils may start by feeling the same way, but would also want to ask more questions. Did other monarchs before and after Mary also order deaths at the stake? Were there other, good things that Mary did as Queen? Can we fairly judge the behaviour of those in the past by the standards we have today? If adolescent pupils still end up believing that Mary was indeed a bad Queen, it will be on the basis of a lot more reasoning than merely reacting to a simple statement. How often adolescents use this new power of thought and in what areas depends on other factors. Most adolescents are capable of considering a number of different hypotheses when trying to explain a problem, such as why a car does not work or why a proposed meeting has failed to take place. But faced with schoolwork that does not engage them, this capacity for abstract thought may simply stay unused.

Adolescents are aware that there is usually more than one way of seeing things. This realization sometimes leads them repeatedly to question their parents' attitudes to various topics. When adults view this new confidence as a challenge to their authority, there can be heated arguments. Even so, with major issues such as moral or political beliefs, most adolescents tend to agree more with their parents than with their friends.

In fact, it has been found that present-day parents disagreed more strongly with their parents over important issues than their own adolescent children now disagree with them (Rutter, 1979). This may be because the largest shifts in attitudes to society, religion, marriage and personal morality took place in Britain during the 1960s. More changes in attitudes have occurred since, but none on quite so vast a scale. It could therefore be expected that greater disagreements between the generations existed 30 years ago than would be true today.

Egocentric errors

The American psychologist David Elkind (1981) describes three **egocentric errors** common during adolescence.

*1. Inability to distinguish between **transient** and **abiding thought**.*
For example: adolescents who think they have made a fool of themselves on one occasion (transient) may be convinced that everyone else will hold this incident against them for ever (abiding).

2. Inability to differentiate between the objective and subjective.
Adolescents obsessed with their bodies, thoughts and feelings sometimes assume that others around them also share this interest. This can lead to a belief in an **imaginary audience**, with self-conscious adolescents assuming that others are always watching and judging what they are doing. Sometimes an adolescent imagines a hostile reaction; sometimes an approving one. So adolescents who show off in company may imagine that an appreciative audience is enjoying the display. Those who behave particularly badly may believe they are getting their own back on an already disapproving audience. They may be confusing the subjective content of their own thoughts (how they feel) with the thoughts of others, who in reality may not be interested in them or in their behaviour.

3. Inability to differentiate the unique from the universal.
Adolescents often imagine they are the only ones to feel or think as they do. This **personal fable** can extend to the idea that because they are unique, rules for others do not apply to them. At worst, this leads to reckless behaviour such as drunk driving or sex without contraceptives. Such actions may be seen as being dangerous only for others since 'Bad things can't happen to me'.

SAQ
4

Describe in your own words the three major errors found in adolescent egocentric thinking.

SOMETHING TO TRY
Write down one example of each type of egocentric thinking from your own experience of adolescence.

Language and environment

Greater intellectual capacity usually brings about an improvement in language skills, with adolescents becoming quicker at understanding irony and less obvious jokes. They are better at conveying their opinions and at listening to, and learning from, what others have to say. Such conversations and sharing of experiences generally lead to a decrease of adolescent **egocentrism** around 15 or 16 years. But intellectual changes do not simply emerge on their own. The environment also exerts a considerable influence. Some cultures value intellectual growth more than others. An atmosphere where open discussion is favoured helps adolescents to explore their new capacity for thinking and argument. Families, schools or social groups that view open discussion with suspicion can prove very constricting, especially for otherwise bright and lively adolescents.

Girls have suffered particularly here, and still do so in social settings where they are not expected to speak up for themselves. Schools that make an effort to treat males and females equally can be particularly helpful. Teachers can ensure that they make the same demands upon both sexes, rather than laying down tough conditions for adolescent males while being less demanding with adolescent females, as sometimes happens (Dweck and Elliot, 1988). Pupils expected to fail soon lose confidence in their own abilities to succeed: a condition known as **learned helplessness**. But girls who are encouraged to ask as many questions as boys benefit from the experience. They also perform well when encouraged to take school subjects once seen as suitable only for males. One study found that female pupils are now doing almost as well as male pupils in mathematics (Hyde and Fennema, 1990).

Adolescents good at their lessons and with a positive attitude towards school, shared by their parents, generally enjoy the extra intellectual demands made upon them at this stage. Those who disliked primary school can still flourish in a good secondary school. But others never settle down into this bigger and more impersonal environment. If these adolescents also possess low attainments and poor attendance records, they may drop out of school altogether, becoming more likely to get involved in **delinquent** activities.

The development of identity

The ability to think in abstract terms makes it possible for adolescents to ponder more deeply about themselves, their parents and the society in which they live. Arriving at a secure sense of identity is not always easy, given that adolescents often change so fast. The American psychoanalyst Erik Erikson (1968) believed that the search for identity is a key feature of adolescence. For him, full individual identity is made up of a number of different factors. *Social* identity is acquired through interaction with friends. A secure *sexual* identity follows when adolescents are able to accept positively the changes going on in their own bodies. An *occupational* identity is acquired once an individual has decided upon a chosen career.

According to Erikson, each adolescent passes through a state of **identity crisis** until they discover the real me. Those who fail to find an acceptable identity for themselves suffer in a number of ways. An adolescent with a **diffused identity** may feel no particular commitment to anything or anybody. Those with a **negative identity** may choose to be someone they don't even like in preference to continuing with the uncertainty of not knowing what sort of person they really are. Some adolescents adopt an identity prematurely suggested to them by friends or by their parents. This early closing down of possibilities for further growth Erikson calls **foreclosure**.

Erikson is only talking about chronic identity diffusion here. He believed that some milder state of identity diffusion is desirable at some time during adolescence. He also thought that most adolescents are prepared to wait to see what sort of person they turn out to be; a period of time he describes as a state of **moratorium**. During this time they often experiment with different roles, behaviours and practices until they arrive at a final sense of **identity achievement**. Erikson believed that adolescents can often acquire a stronger sense of identity after having successfully weathered an earlier crisis of identity confusion.

But adolescents who remain quite unable to synthesise the various different influences bearing upon them into one stable personality risk drifting into a state of moral confusion. This is because they have no consistent set of internal standards with which to judge their own or other people's behaviour. The absence of an integrated sense of themselves can lead them to take up unrealistic career choices. They may also, in Erikson's opinion, develop a general sense of cynicism as a disguise for their own inner state of confusion.

Psychologists have found Erikson's ideas about identity formation useful in helping to explain many adolescents' preoccupations with who they are and who they would like to be. But not all adolescents have an identity crisis. Again, different people have different experiences. Adolescents who talk about their feelings with family or friends are more likely to develop a positive sense of self. For others, a large difference between their ideal self and the way they perceive themselves to be may lead to self-doubt. In developing his ideas, Erikson drew heavily upon literature and biography as well as on his own experience of working with disturbed adolescents and adults. The theories he advanced were therefore derived from a comparatively small and atypical selection of cases.

Even so, this theory has had a major impact upon how we think about the whole of life development. Instead of focusing only on childhood, Erikson suggested that there are eight equally important stages throughout life, each of which must be resolved **psychosocially**. So while adolescence is strongly associated with physical change, it is a period of life made more easy or more difficult by how well these changes are accepted by friends, parents and the rest of society.

Erikson's model for life-long developmental change (Erikson, 1968) is shown in Figure 3. Each interconnected stage is linked with a set of psychosocial crises which the individual has to solve in order to proceed satisfactorily to the next stage. Infants, for example, should be in a position to trust their environment. Given stable, loving parenting, they should be able to develop a habit of hope that will take them satisfactorily up to the next, toddler stage. But if they only learn mistrust at this first stage, their chance of developing a sense of **autonomy** through the positive application of their will power at Stage 2 will be less. Instead, they may feel a lack of self-confidence and a sense of shame about themselves.

Once at old age, individuals may arrive at a state of **wisdom** based on the positive feelings arising out of a state of **ego integrity**. On the other hand, they may instead succumb to a general sense of **despair**. If they go this last way, Erikson assumes it will be because they very often came out negatively at the seven other stages they were faced with before.

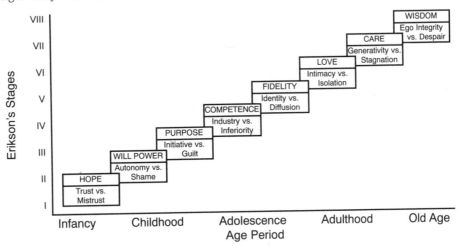

FIGURE 3. *Erikson's model of developmental change.* From Lamb and Bornstein (1988)

Where his ideas on adolescence are concerned, it may be relevant that Erikson never knew his own father and later repudiated the name of his German step-father. In creating his own name for himself, 'Erik, son of Erik,' he revealed that the search for identity was certainly of great importance in his own life. Striking and persuasive as Erikson's ideas are, it should always be remembered that many adolescents, either in Western society or elsewhere in the Third World, do not necessarily go through such difficulties in self-realization.

SAQ
5

Describe what Erikson saw as unhealthy solutions to identity crises.

Social changes

Most adolescents do not want to be treated as children. They need some independence and usually want to make more decisions for themselves. This may lead to tension at home over issues such as dress, bedtime and coming home late. Such issues can usually be settled, although most people can remember having some big arguments. Even so, approximately three-quarters of adolescents questioned in a survey said they approved of their parents' approach to discipline, and many named their parents when asked whom they most admired.

In another survey, only 12 per cent of adolescent boys and 7 per cent of adolescent girls reported regularly retreating to their rooms or staying out of the house in an effort to get away from the rest of their family. Ninety per cent of 16-year-olds said they got on well with their mothers and 75 per cent said the same about their fathers. Only a quarter of college students remembered their own adolescence as a strongly rebellious period (Nicholson, 1980).

Those adolescents who are allowed to do exactly what they like do not seem to benefit from having total freedom. It is important for parents to know roughly where their children are and what they are doing at any particular time. Vandalism, drug-taking and sexual promiscuity are more likely to occur when there are no parental rules. Parental support and encouragement also have a positive effect on schoolwork (Rutter *et al.* 1979).

But even with the best will possible, it is not always easy for parents to know what their adolescent children may be going through. Rutter *et al* (1976) found, in a survey, that while up to a third of teenagers reported feelings of depression, only a few parents ever acknowledged that adolescent children might occasionally feel depressed. It is natural for most parents not to want to think their children are sometimes miserable, but this type of parental denial does not help those adolescents needing extra support at what might be a difficult time of their lives.

Adolescents benefit when they have a supportive group of friends. Such friendships are not based only on shared activities as before; adolescents now tend to exchange confidences and share their feelings. Girls usually have more intense same-sex friendships, while boys often prefer a looser-knit group of friends. A close social group allows for a sense of belonging and promotes self-confidence.

For Coleman and Hendry (1990), the **peer group** 'supports independence, meets needs for identity and recognition, presents opportunities for achievement, and affords the opportunity of playing a variety of quasi-adult roles' (p.138). Individual adolescents often complain of shyness and social inhibition; acceptance by their peer group can greatly help to develop their own perspectives and self-confidence. Seeing how older adolescents deal with new social situations can suggest techniques to younger peers which they too may want to try out in time.

Within the peer group, conversational ease usually rates high, together with an ability to share the feelings of others. As adolescents get older, the larger peer group tends to become less important as they concentrate more on fewer, closer relationships. Those adolescents who have never been fully accepted by their peer group may experience a sense of loneliness. They may also have missed a chance to learn valuable social skills.

But although adolescents generally spend more leisure time with friends than with families, they still tend to be more concerned about causing their parents' disapproval than they are about disagreements with their friends. Most adolescents maintain close ties with their parents even while gaining new independence. Those who seriously fall out with their parents are a minority who are likely to have experienced problems at home before.

SAQ
6

To what extent are parents and adolescents likely to disagree?

Adolescents with unhappy childhoods may continue to be unhappy for the same reasons, for example, family tension or general deprivation and neglect. A deprived neighbourhood is more conducive to truancy, delinquency or experimentation with hard drugs. Supportive relationships at school make a big difference. For example, a teacher taking a particular interest can provide valuable help for an otherwise discontented and frustrated pupil.

Sexual changes

Hormonal changes and the greater production of **androgens** (male sex hormones) lead to increased sexual desire, particularly among males. Sexual interest is usually but not always directed towards the opposite sex. In a survey of 14- to 15-year-olds, 29 per cent of girls and 14 per cent of boys admitted to having a special friend of the opposite sex. But first love relationships tend to be brief, and can cause considerable unhappiness when they are ruptured.

One in five British under-sixteens appear to be sexually active, with the average age of first sexual intercourse now 17 (Wellings *et al.* 1994). Another survey suggests that while 60 per cent of 15- to 19-year-olds were sexually active, 13 per cent of those aged 14 and under had also had sexual intercourse (Kruss, 1992).

According to Hayes (1987), early sexual activity is associated with:

- low intellectual ability
- poor parent/child relationships
- a broken home, serious family disorganization or a single-parent family
- a mother who also became sexually active very early on
- involvement with other less approved adult activities such as smoking and heavy drinking
- poverty.

15

Inadequate parental control, poverty and a lack of positive adult models are also associated with a wide cluster of other social problems. Early adolescent sexual activity may often be a symptom of the more general deprivation suffered by adolescents growing up in a situation of neglect.

Girls who fail to use contraceptives are also more likely to have low intelligence and poor family relationships. On the other hand, girls who use contraceptives regularly generally have higher self-esteem and start sexual activities at a later age within a committed relationship.

Adolescent girls who become pregnant and decide to have the baby may do so partly to escape from an unrewarding family situation. They may not feel in control of their lives, seeing themselves as being at the mercy of fate. Pregnancy also tends to go with dropping out of school and a decline in material standards of living. Further unintended births are not unlikely. Should marriage take place, it is often to someone who is unskilled and who comes from the same type of disadvantaged background. There is a high risk of marital breakdown later on, especially when the marriage mainly takes place as a result of an unplanned pregnancy (Furstenberg *et al.* 1987).

Furstenberg and his colleagues came to this finding while researching the subsequent careers of 300 American teenage mothers. They discovered that two thirds of the mothers' first marriages and over half of their second marriages had broken down in a period stretching over 17 years. Some of the mothers were still receiving welfare, but these were a minority. Others were now in work and had often received more education. It was only their marital stability that was worse than average over the whole sample.

Teenage pregnancies with a better outcome seem to depend on:
• parental support and good material circumstances
• good personal competence and high educational aspirations
• completion of school and/or further education
• avoidance of further unplanned births
• appropriate career decisions.

Adolescents who have abortions tend to be better educated and to have greater self-esteem. Psychological disorder after abortion is not common, occurring less than is the case after normal childbirth.

Emotional changes

Adolescents often take themselves very seriously, and expect others to do the same. But problems that seem enormous at the time often become more manageable once an adolescent realizes that many others experience some of the same feelings too. Special provision for adolescents, such as a personal tutor system at school or the availability of counselling make life easier should an adolescent wish to consult someone outside the family. A general understanding, within the family as well as outside, that adolescence can be a time for occasional mood swings will also help.

Adolescents may have some experience of depression, occasionally coupled with fears about their own futures. Such episodes of general sadness are common throughout life, and are not peculiar to adolescence. In a few cases, adolescents experience quite serious depressive disorders. It is possible that hormonal changes make some of them more vulnerable to various types of depression. There is also an increase in schizophrenic breakdown during this time, again only affecting a few adolescents. The reason why such disorders first show themselves during adolescence remains unclear.

Inward-looking adolescents given to depression often have a harder time dealing with their emotions. Family disruption, change of school or illness also make life hard. At an extreme level, an unhappy adolescent may attempt suicide. Although the numbers are small, suicide attempts and suicide itself are increasing among this young population (Rutter and Rutter, 1992). While suicide is almost unheard of before the age of 10, there is a large increase in the suicide rate between 10 and 20.

(?) *Why do you think more serious depressive disorders first appear during adolescence?*

Individual variations

Temperament	Some people are born with more anxious and irritable natures than others.
Family history	Some families are more supportive than others. Yet members of the same family can still feel differently according to temperamental factors and relationships within the family.
Physique	Adolescents who feel healthy and attractive will feel more self-confident than those who dislike their own physical appearance. Adolescents with physical disabilities may have particular problems when it comes to be accepted by their peer group. Those from minority groups may experience racial prejudice and have a harder time in an unsympathetic social environment (Daniel, 1968).
Abilities and aptitudes	Some adolescents find school work easier than others. Others discover particular talents, for example in sports or the arts. In both cases, this can greatly enhance self-image.
Socio-economic background	Adolescents from a settled and supportive background have the opportunity to benefit from this stability. Those with educated parents also have the extra benefit of help with schoolwork. Adolescents from deprived backgrounds involving poverty, bad housing or inadequate parenting have more of a struggle. Those in institutional care can find life particularly difficult.

Locality	A prosperous suburb offers a different experience to living in a tough inner-city area. Life in the deep countryside is different in other ways. Adolescents coming from such varied backgrounds are bound to be influenced by the social, economic and geographic differences existing between their various backgrounds.
Friends	A supportive group of friends is a great source of strength to an adolescent. But other groups can encourage **anti-social** behaviour such as alcohol or drug abuse.
Life events, or pure luck	An adolescent life can be changed radically by some unexpected event. The death of a parent, a serious illness or accident, a bitter divorce or a parent's unemployment can all unsettle an adolescent. Whether he or she recovers will depend upon their already existing strengths and weaknesses, and on how well they are supported within and outside the family.

These different combinations of personal and social factors make it impossible to talk about a 'typical' adolescent. There are typical adolescent experiences, but what each person makes of these is always an individual matter.

Adulthood and old age

KEY AIMS: By the end of Part 2 you will be able to:
▷   trace normal adult development from 18 years to old age
▷   assess the impact of work, marriage, parenting and divorce
▷   assess the impact of retirement, bereavement and the knowledge of one's own imminent death.

Adulthood: 18 to 40

Until recently, adulthood was said to begin at 21. Today, the age of majority starts at 18; from this time, parental legal rights over children disappear. In reality, these particular ages mean little, with each individual progressing towards maturity in his or her own way. An independent adolescent can sometimes seem more adult than an over-protected son or daughter in their twenties still living at home. But there are some changes common to most young adults, although what each one makes of them may be very different.

Physical changes

Muscular strength is at its peak between 20 and 30 years. Older athletes must therefore concentrate on skills of endurance rather than try to compete for speed and agility. For example, top sprinters rarely win tournaments over the age of 30, but long-distance runners continue winning well after that. A slight decline in vision and hearing starts around 25, and the skin gradually begins to lose moisture. Blood pressure rises from 30 years onwards, and weight also tends to increase; two excellent reasons for continuing to take regular exercise in order to stay healthy.

Intellectual changes

'Fluid' intelligence is the ability to think at speed. This is measured in tests demanding mental agility and is at its peak in early adulthood. **'Crystallized' intelligence** reveals itself in knowledge of past experience and the ability to apply this to the present. As Figure 4 shows, this type of intelligence can continue to grow until old age and is most obvious in individuals who are specialists in particular fields of knowledge. It is best measured in tests of vocabulary, comprehension and general knowledge. Fluid intelligence is revealed in skill when tackling tricky 'brain-teasing' types of question (Cattell, 1971). This does tend to show a decline with age.

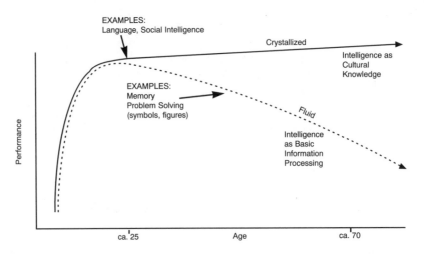

FIGURE 4. *Different forms of intelligence.* From Lamb and Bornstein (1988)

In general, intelligence levels stay constant between adolescence and adulthood. There is a slight slowing down in performance on timed tests after the age of 25, but reasoning ability often improves during adulthood. Adults also have more experience to draw upon, and more time in which to have developed effective ways of dealing with a variety of demands and tasks. But the overall pattern of intellectual change in adulthood is also an individual matter, improving during periods of study at any age and slackening off when life becomes routinely predictable. Rabbitt and Goward (1994) suggest that any decline in intelligence through age tends to be more rapid among people who are already not particularly intelligent. Highly intelligent individuals, by contrast, tend to suffer a less marked decline in **IQ** with age.

Emotional changes

According to a British survey, unmarried adults in their twenties usually want to spend as much time as possible with people their own age (Nicholson, 1980). But they also have an intense interest in themselves, sometimes feeling threatened by others who seem to be encroaching on their inner space by getting too close or by making too many demands. This particular tension has been called by Erikson (1968) the 'intimacy versus isolation' crisis, since there is usually a need for emotionally close relationships as well as for independence at this age.

Those who are able to disclose their personal feelings to others and who are also prepared to listen when others are doing the same are more likely to have satisfactory emotional relationships. But such disclosures are best done in moderation. People who reveal every detail of their emotional life may prove very tiring to others. Those who refuse to say anything at all come over as extremely defensive. In either event, emotional disclosure seems to work best in a relationship when both individuals involved discuss their feelings in equal measure (Nicholson, 1980).

Do you agree with Erikson that a particular conflict facing people in their twenties is 'intimacy versus isolation'?

For some young adults, freedom from parental dominance leads to insecurity. A really secure sense of identity may not be established until the early thirties and some individuals in their twenties still have nagging worries about who they are and what they want from life. Such concerns can make the twenties an awkward time, particularly when it comes to taking important decisions with serious implications for the future, like marriage or choice of job. Yet when asked, more older people say they would rather return to their twenties than to their teens (Nicholson, 1980).

The greatest impact upon adults comes not from biological changes – since adolescence these are greatly slowing down and in general becoming much more gradual – but from changes arising from interaction with the outside world, in particular in relation to employment.

Work and unemployment

Apart from providing an income and social contacts, work plays an important role in the individual's sense of personal worth, both to themselves and to others. For Professor Marie Jahoda: 'First, employment imposes a time structure on the working day; second, employment implies regular shared experiences and contacts with people outside the nuclear family; third, employment links people to goals and purposes that transcend their own; fourth, employment defines aspects of personal status and identity; and finally, employment enforces activity' (quoted in Rutter and Rutter, 1992).

Much also depends upon the nature of the work involved. While high-powered jobs may be good for self-esteem, they can also be more stressful. In one survey of working men, 55 per cent of professional workers reported job-related strain compared with only 15 per cent of unskilled workers (Cherry, 1984). More permanent dissatisfaction with jobs tends to be caused by:

- lack of control over work activities
- lack of opportunity to exercise skills
- lack of variety in work tasks
- very high job demands
- unpleasant work environment
- lack of sense of direction
- poor personal relationships.

AGED 25 While work can provide great personal satisfaction, unfavourable work conditions may lead to unhappiness and at times to mental health problems. Failure to get promotion may cause bitterness, but promotion that entails harder demands or an unwelcome move can also lead to stress.

Women with children often welcome the chance to work, but tend to worry about neglecting family responsibilities far more than do most fathers in work.

I'M FAR TOO YOUNG TO BE WORRYING ABOUT A PENSION.

21

What do you think are the most important factors leading to work satisfaction?

In 1933, a classic study was made of the effects of unemployment on an Austrian village named Marienthal (Jahoda *et al*, 1971). Its main findings have been replicated many times since in subsequent research. What Jahoda and her colleagues found was a strong link between long-term unemployment, depressed passivity and low self-esteem. Individuals existed in a state of drifting without any positive expectations for the future. They often made less effort to look for work even when it was available, so great was their expectation of failure. While unemployed parents often kept things neat and tidy at home, marital problems frequently increased as did mental and physical health problems. The unemployed also felt cut off from the wider community, staying within their own homes feeling isolated and useless. Time was passed aimlessly, often with little fixed pattern as day followed day. Odd bouts of violence sometimes occurred, or else moments of irrational spending, even when money was already short.

Jahoda and her colleagues also suggest that the young often come to share the depressed attitudes of their unemployed parents. In general, the children of Marienthal expected much less from life than did children living in areas of higher employment. When asked about their own likely job prospects, they seemed prepared for joblessness themselves when the time came. The older the child, the more they feared for their future. They also tended to be more passive in their attitudes, and less inclined to join in communal activities.

Older adults with good levels of social and financial support usually survive unemployment better. Ways of coping effectively include keeping contact with others outside the family, maintaining a degree of activity and accepting the fact of unemployment while it lasts.

With younger adults, unemployment tends to lead to an increase in delinquency. Frustration with poverty and a low status in society help to explain the fact that crimes committed for material gain always increase with the growth of unemployment (West, 1982). But such crimes are also more likely to be committed by people with a previous history of delinquency. A record of difficult behaviour and low intelligence further predisposes an unemployed person to crime.

Marriage and intimate relationships

Similarity and compatibility seem the best predictors for a successful long-term relationship. Shared intellectual interests, physical closeness, good communication and the approval of family and friends also play a positive part. Each couple will have different ideas on which of these factors they think most important, with close agreement here another positive sign for the couple's future.

The success of any marriage tends to depend more on the personality of the husband than on that of the wife. There are more men who are disturbed or aggressive than there are women. While some wives will be 'difficult ' too, the indication is that within marriage women are far more likely than men to accommodate their partner's needs (Bernard, 1982). Moderate affluence is also a great help, with many marriages coming apart when there is not enough money to go round.

The most popular age for getting married or setting up a long-term relationship in the UK is between 20 and 24. After marriage, both partners tend to become less sociable and more attentive to each other. Men, in general, greatly benefit from marriage, usually remaining in better health physically and mentally than single men of the same age. They also tend to live longer and have more successful careers.

SAQ 7

Is the attraction of opposites a good basis for long-term relationships?

Women may have more problems within marriage, particularly when they have children. Trying to pursue a career while taking care of small children is extremely difficult, but staying at home full-time can lead to frustration and boredom. There is no good reason why women should take on most of the burdens of child care but, culturally, the expectation that they should do so remains strong. Up to 90 per cent of women in their thirties have children for whom they usually take chief responsibility.

Some seriously delinquent young adults make a fresh start with marriage, settling down into a more respectable life-style. But if a delinquent adult sets up home with a spouse or partner sharing similar habits and perhaps drawn from the same criminally-minded social group, little or no improvement can be expected. Sadly, many disturbed or delinquent young adults often do choose spouses or partners sharing similar problems and outlooks.

It is difficult in general to predict why some previously disturbed or delinquent young adults eventually settle down while others go on to a life of crime. As Rutter (1989) has shown, the particular pathway taken by each individual is always a combination of different genetic, environmental, cognitive and personality influences. But the nature and timing of particular experiences such as marriage may always give some individuals the chance to 'make good'.

SAQ 8

Can marriage put young adults with anti-social tendencies back on the right track?

Parenting

Attempting to explain why some parents manage better with their children than others, Belsky (1984) suggests that good parenting is determined by the interaction of three important factors. From an investigation of existing research, he concludes that the psychological state of the parent is an important factor in determining how sensitively they bring up their children. A parent's personal maturity and sense of psychological well-being will also have a powerful effect on the second important factor mentioned by Belsky: those external sources of support available to a parent, such as marital relationships and social networks. Such sources can provide valuable emotional support and practical assistance; they can also help parents form high social expectations about how they should best exert their responsibilities when bringing up their children.

Belsky also discusses the effect of the child itself, and his or her particular characteristics: the last of the three main factors he considers when discussing good parenting. A child with an easy temperament causes less parental stress than a child who seems born difficult. But weighing all these three factors together, Belsky concludes that the positive psychological resources of a parent make up the most important factor in successfully bringing up a child, followed by the quality of the sources of support parents can call upon. The characteristics of the child seem least important in explaining good parenting, providing the parent has a healthy personality and receives adequate support, for example from friends, spouse and their own family network.

Pregnancy itself can be a healthy and a happy time for women looking forward to having a baby, but it can also bring new stresses. There may be anxiety about whether the baby will be born normal. At another level, some women feel concern about spoiling their career prospects. Mothers-to-be can be greatly helped by a supportive husband or partner, although most men take some time before becoming really interested in their partner's pregnancy. Marital difficulties or existing psychological problems in either partner may become more severe during pregnancy.

Once the baby is born, pleasure and pride in creating a new life can draw parents together. Having a young child makes divorce less likely in the early years of marriage, and couples with children of any age divorce on average half as often as do childless couples. But even when all is well, only 25 per cent of couples report gains in their marriage, and more report some negative effects (Rutter and Rutter, 1992). Parenting means giving up some independence and spending longer hours at home, and while this can be satisfying it can also be frustrating, particularly for mothers if they do most of the child-rearing. Shortage of money is often an issue when trying to bring up a family, and interrupted sleep can lead to irritability in both partners.

It is difficult to predict who will be good parents. Special care is needed to get over a difficult birth or to bring up a baby with a disability. Parents who have little skill in child management may have a stressful time. Young children need firm boundaries and consistency from their parents. Adults who have had unhappy childhoods themselves sometimes find it extra hard to give their own children the love which they were once denied in their own lives. But again, these might be the very people who, in the right circumstances, may be determined to give their children what they themselves never enjoyed. Poverty and over-crowding give rise to particular problems. Parents with good jobs, acceptable housing conditions and plenty of support in their wider community generally have a better chance of enjoying and providing for their children.

Other factors associated with successful parenting include: knowing how to talk to and play with children; the ability to have positive social relationships in general; good mental health and previous successful experience in parenting.

A second child may have an easier time as parents now know more about what they are doing and are therefore more relaxed. But the temperament of the baby is also important. Difficult children can drain the emotional and physical resources of the most well-meaning parents – particularly in situations where good external support for the parents is lacking.

SOMETHING TO TRY
List what you see as the main advantages and disadvantages of having children.

Divorce

Some marriages hardly get off the ground, with serious problems starting almost immediately. This happens most frequently when couples marry after discovering an unwanted pregnancy without building on any real evidence of compatibility. Separation and divorce after a longer marriage usually implies a more gradual growing apart. Possible indicators for marriage breakdown include:

- Serious behaviour problems in a partner's childhood.
- Partners who were brought up in unhappy homes and/or whose own parents divorced.

AGED 35

NO, I DON'T HAVE A PENSION PLAN.

- Psychiatric problems.
- Poverty and inadequate housing.
- Early marriage.
- A shorter than average courtship before marriage.

The first year after divorce tends to be the most difficult for all concerned. If children are involved, parental skills sometimes deteriorate. Should poverty and worse housing conditions follow divorce these too bring new strains. But if there is good communication between parents themselves and their children, different members of the family may eventually settle down to their new situation, sometimes coming to welcome the divorce should it also mean a release from upsetting family quarrels. Even so, the marital stress that can lead to separation and divorce may still be deeply upsetting to all concerned. Divorcees have a higher suicide rate than married people, and are more prone to mental and physical illness. Yet about half of all divorcees marry again within a year of their divorce, and three-quarters find a new spouse within three years. But the divorce rate for second marriages also remains high, especially for those who first married while still teenagers.

Social conditions

A booming economy offers hope and support to young adults, whereas high unemployment can lead to hopelessness and despair. Racial discrimination works against black adults who still have the lowest chance of getting a job. Young adults from ethnic minorities may also experience conflict between conventional standards and the norms of their own cultures. This can cause problems, for example, when parents plan for an arranged marriage against the wishes of their now grown-up children. Homosexual men and women may also find life hard, depending on how much prejudice there is in their local community.

There is also always the element of luck. Meeting the right person at the right time, securing a satisfying job, or having children who become a source of deep pleasure all make life easier. But a child who is seriously disabled, a bad accident, illness or an unexpected redundancy can unsettle any couple, particularly if there are already other problems. Luck, both good and bad, makes a huge difference to life as it is and how it is going to develop in the next phase of adulthood.

Adulthood: 40 to 60

Middle-age is a time for adapting to the idea that one is no longer young. This can be harder for some than for others, particularly those in jobs where youth is important, such as sport, acting or modelling. For others, middle-age may be a time of opportunity: politicians, barristers and teachers seldom get maximum promotion before the age of 40.

AGED 45

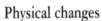

Physical changes

Illness and disability increase during this time, but the frequency of accidents goes down. Older adults are less likely to get common colds, but they do tire more easily. Muscular strength tends to decline, except for those who keep exercising. In general, movements get slower and hearing and eyesight deteriorate. Rapid physical decline in this period

UNFORTUNATELY, I HAVEN'T BEEN ABLE TO START A PENSION.

is often due to illness or avoidable physical abuse, such as smoking, drinking too much or general inactivity. A fit 60-year-old can still do hard physical work, although usually at half the speed achieved 40 years earlier.

The wisdom derived from life experience helps an older person compensate for reduced physical strength and attractiveness. Younger people often turn to their elders for advice, while older people may be less influenced by the opinions of others, preferring instead to form and follow their own judgements.

Intellectual changes

There is some evidence of a general mental slowing down during this time, but there are large individual differences. For example, a survey found no significant intellectual decline in 33 per cent of individuals regularly tested between the ages of 23 and 53 (Schaie and Willis, 1986).

In general, middle-aged adults continue to perform as well as younger people. The more use they make of their intelligence the less likely it is to decline. For some, however, handling new and difficult information at speed gets harder, yet vocabulary can continue to increase up to the mid-fifties. Short-term memory may deteriorate slightly, but it tends to stay at what it was around the age of 40 until the onset of extreme old age.

Emotional changes

A phrase used in connection with people in their late forties and fifties is 'mid-life crisis', their supposed reaction to the feeling of fast disappearing youth and the belief that many of life's options have finally closed. But there is no real evidence of any particular mental turmoil during this period. As with adolescents, a minority may have a difficult time but many adults find this a good period of life.

The **menopause** has also been described as a crisis time for women. It has been associated with hot flushes, headaches, sleeplessness and weight increase. Around 10% of women do find this a troubling time physically, but 25 per cent report no adverse symptoms. The menopause has also been thought to cause problems of self-confidence, with women unwilling to face up to this evidence of loss of youth. Yet in surveys, only 10 per cent of women regret reaching this stage (Nicholson, 1980). Some women discover a new interest in sex now there is no danger of conception, but others have difficulties in continuing with sex for its own sake once there is no possibility of bearing a child.

The male sex drive tends to lessen during this period, but again there is much individual variation. A new sexual relationship can renew this drive, particularly if the man concerned has entered into it as one way of denying the fact of his own ageing. Within stable marriages, sexual interest is likely to decline more rapidly among males than females, and this can lead to problems.

SAQ
9

Is middle age necessarily a time of crisis?

Social changes

As active parenting draws to a close, adults have more time for life outside the home. Mothers no longer tied to their children may want to go out more. This may coincide with a stage when their husbands start taking things easier, preferring to spend more time at home. Tensions may rise unless this particular division of interests is resolved. But it is interesting to note that only 10 per cent of all divorces take place between 50 and 60.

In stable marriages, sex may now play a less important role than sociability and sharing common interests. Men in particular are often very satisfied with their marriages in their fifties, saying they feel closer to their wives than before. Women may have new energy once their children have left home, and do not always seem quite so satisfied with their husbands. But by the end of their fifties, both partners often express equal satisfaction (Rollins and Feldman, 1970).

Some mothers may particularly miss their children who have left home – the 'empty nest' syndrome. But unless it is a marriage that has only stayed together because of the children, in which case it may quickly disintegrate, marital satisfaction often increases when children leave. One reason for this is that parents worry less about their children once they have left school and secured a job. Arguments between parents about children, a common cause of tension, also tend to stop at this stage.

Children are very expensive, particularly as they get older. Once they have gone, there is usually more money for parents to enjoy for themselves. Older children who refuse to leave home can cause a different sort of crisis – the so-called 'full nest syndrome' – when parents start resenting their adult children's continuing dependence upon them.

What do you think are the advantages and disadvantages for parents when children finally leave home?

During this period of life, adults often have to help look after their own ageing parents. In a survey, 33 per cent of adults spoke positively about their old parents, but another third resented having to take some responsibility for them.

At work, adults stand most chance of promotion in their forties and of being made redundant in their fifties. For both sexes, a satisfying job is still of major importance, particularly for women whose children have grown up. People who have become top management executives may find more satisfaction in work now they have high status. But those of the same age working in more subordinate positions, attribute less importance to work in their lives. Men who do manual work may now find it increasingly difficult to keep up, which can become a source of strain.

AGED 55

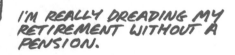

I'M REALLY DREADING MY RETIREMENT WITHOUT A PENSION.

Old age: 60 plus

Old age can be divided into four stages, corresponding to the four decades between 60 and 100. How people cope with life at each of these stages is again an individual matter, with much depending on the changes and life events they experience.

Physical changes

Eighty-five per cent of adults over 65 suffer from at least one chronic illness such as arthritis or rheumatism. But older adults who remain in good health can lead vigorous lives. While muscles shrink and bones become more fragile, those adults who have always taken plenty of exercise stay relatively strong. Sexual activity can last into the eighties, depending on the health of both partners.

The difference in quality of life between a fit and an ill old person may be extreme. In fact, much of the decline that can happen with old age has more to do with the effects of various prolonged and weakening illnesses rather than anything to do with old age as such.

Intellectual changes

Old age is commonly associated with a decline in mental ability, yet only around 5 per cent of adults are forced to end their days in institutional care. Although not as fast in their mental responses as previously, older people can still perform successfully where learning skills are concerned. Some choose to study, and others remain lively and alert by taking an active interest in life.

Alzheimer's disease sometimes occurs during this stage. This involves changes in brain structure which result in the gradual disintegration of function with severe effects upon the intellect. Alzheimer's disease occurs in 5 per cent of 70-year-olds, though this figure increases to 15 per cent of 80-year-olds and 30 per cent of 90-year-olds. The percentage of elderly people with poor mental health is similar to that of the rest of the population.

Emotional and social changes

Most older people find grandparenting easier than parenting, and often derive great pleasure from it. Grandparents themselves range in age from under 40 to past 100. Many younger grandparents still go to work and are not always easily available to grandchildren. An American survey found that 60 per cent of grandparents see their grandchildren once or twice a month, although such visits decline as the grandchildren grow older. Thirty-three per cent of grandmothers rated their relationship with their grandchildren as 'very important,' but another 25 per cent had no involvement (Neugarten and Weinstein, 1964).

Stable and contented marriages remain important at this age, particularly when it comes to avoiding the problem of loneliness. An American study found that 90 per cent of older married couples described their relationship as very good. But older people on their own face a greater possibility of loneliness in old age. From the late teens onwards, social networks tend to reduce in the life of most individuals. Old age can occasionally leave people with few friends plus diminishing energy and confidence in their ability to form new social contacts (Dickens and Perlman, 1981).

SOMETHING TO TRY
Think about the relationships you have or have had with your grandparents. How satisfying and meaningful have these been, both to you and to them?

Many older people become more introverted with age, voluntarily disengaging themselves from social activities and preferring to stay at home. But for some, it remains important to keep links with the wider community, staying active and deriving satisfaction from continual social contact with others.

In these cases, a supportive community offering a wide range of opportunities can help make old age for some a happy and creative time. But if resources are limited, with older people sometimes afraid to go out because of high levels of street crime, depression can follow. This may be especially true for those who find their usual links with the community, which had normally served them well, involuntarily severed by a retirement they did not welcome or by the death of a spouse. A community that does not value its older members cannot be surprised if older people react negatively themselves, sometimes by the type of poor mental or physical health that might have been avoided given more positive circumstances.

(?) *Does old age have to be a largely depressing time of life?*

The suicide rate for people over 65 is three times that of the general population. The suicide rate for males peaks in the eighties; for females it peaks in the fifties and then declines. The death of a spouse, entry into an institution, major illness, becoming unemployed or divorce can all cause the type of severe depression that occasionally leads to suicide.

Factors likely to lead to a satisfying old age include good health; good family relationships in childhood; no psychiatric problems; a sound, practical approach to life; no over-dependence on alcohol or drugs such as tranquillizers; plenty of exercise in early life; a stable marriage; adequate material circumstances.

AGED 65   ## Retirement

While some individuals react badly to retirement, many more seem to enjoy it and occasionally even improve in health. The following factors are associated with successful retirement:

NOW I'VE RETIRED, I DON'T KNOW HOW I'M GOING TO SURVIVE.

1. Retirement at the expected age. This is easier to accept and prepare for than is forced or unexpected retirement.
2. Retirement from a stressful, unpleasant job, as opposed to leaving a good, satisfying job.
3. Adequate funds.
4. The ability to develop new friends and interests.
5. A stable marriage which can withstand spending a lot of time in each other's company.

SAQ 10

Dr Alex Comfort has described the popular stereotype of old people as: 'Unintelligent, unemployable, crazy and asexual'. Are such stereotypes true?

Death and bereavement

The death of a spouse is usually a very stressful event during old age. Men often seem more affected than women, possibly because they often have fewer friends outside the house and therefore no social group to turn to for support. Intense grief reactions can last for up to two years, although such reactions tend to be less when death is expected and comes from natural causes. But the death rate among old people who have been widowed is ten times the rate for people of the same age who are still married (Bahr and Peterson, 1989).

There are many reasons why some old people live longer than others. Good health is obviously important, plus the means necessary to live free from material hardship. In addition, the age at which one's own parents died is often an indicator of how long one might live oneself. Biological sex is important too; females on average live seven years longer than males.

There is also the more general issue of quality of life. Active, cheerful and popular old people are much less prone to depression than those who are solitary and lonely, and depression is often linked with decreased resistance to mental and physical illness. The degree to which older people still feel responsible and in control of their own lives has a powerful effect on every aspect of health. Steps should be taken whenever possible to counter feelings of dependence and inadequacy.

Very old people, increasingly surrounded by the deaths of their contemporaries, may feel lonely and depressed, although there may be some satisfaction as well as guilt in the idea that they are still alive when many others are not. People who show the greatest anxiety about dying are often those who are uncertain about what happens after death. Kalish (1985) reports that fear of death is least among both the deeply religious

AGED 66

THANK GOD I DIDN'T BOTHER!

and the deeply irreligious. Elizabeth Kübler-Ross (1969), who worked for many years with terminally ill people described the following reactions to knowledge of one's own imminent death:

1. *Denial*: 'Not me!'
2. *Anger*: 'Why me?'
3. *Bargaining*. The individual tries to make some deal with fate: 'If you will just let me live another year ...'
4. *Depression*. This can happen when symptoms become too obvious to ignore; there may also be a great sense of loss.
5. *Acceptance*. If the depression lifts, it can be replaced by a sense of detachment as individuals quietly anticipate their own departure.

Not everyone experiences all these stages in this particular order. But those older people who are more content and who have already lived through the deaths of their contemporaries are often more prepared for their own death when it comes. People who feel they are still too young, or else that life has never yielded them the satisfactions that they hoped for, may instead feel generally bitter during their last days.

Old people who maintain active relationships during the last years of life tend to survive longer than those with poor social relationships. Shortly before a natural death there is often a sudden drop in intellectual performance. This can make it less likely for an old person to spend their last months worrying about ultimate issues of life and death. More often, they remain preoccupied with ordinary daily concerns (Kübler-Ross, 1969).

Human development and individual variation

Human beings are born, mature and eventually die. Most also go to work, get married and have children. But despite these common factors we all lead very different lives. Some of this variation can be traced to the temperament and personality of individuals themselves, some to their upbringing and some to the environment in which they live. In all human development, inherited biological factors constantly interact with social and cultural variables.

Biological factors

Physique

A strong, healthy person has more immediate advantages than someone who is frail or seriously disabled. Disfigurement, especially facial, is likely to bring about negative responses. Certain skin colours can arouse prejudice and discrimination, particularly when it comes to getting a job.

Temperament

Babies are born with marked individual differences. Some seem naturally shy and diffident, backing away from new situations in favour of the familiar. Children who remain painfully shy are more likely to develop anxiety disorders when older. Children who are difficult about sleeping and eating and generally negative in mood often receive more criticism at home and later at school than do others. This can lead to low personal expectations and self-esteem. At extreme levels, children who show high levels of anti-social behaviour may be more at risk of becoming delinquent when older. As adults, the same individuals have a greater than average tendency to lose their jobs through quarrelling; they are also more likely to divorce. The link between hyperactivity, conduct disturbance and poor peer relations in childhood with serious disturbance or criminality in the adult years is particularly strong (Rutter, 1989).

The extent to which temperamental characteristics are inherited is not clear. **Genetic** factors account for 30 per cent to 60 per cent of variation between individuals. Adopted children have been found to have nearly four times greater than average risk of developing alcohol or anti-social problems in later life if their biological relatives also suffered from the same problems (Rutter, 1989). But environmental influences are important too. Hodges and Tizard (1989) studied a group of children reared in residential nurseries who were then either restored to their parents or else adopted into stable, harmonious homes. The children re-united with their parents showed a high rate of anti-social behaviour later on, which was not surprising given that their families were often disturbed and disadvantaged. The children adopted into 'good' homes were much less likely to show this anti-social pattern, although they still tended to be more worried, unhappy and fearful than other children of the same age.

With the possible exceptions of autism and schizophrenia, psychiatric disorders do not seem to be inherited. Individuals may inherit a predisposition towards characteristics like placidity, anxiety, good humour or high levels of aggression. But how family and society react to an individual will be as important as that person's inborn temperament in determining how he or she will experience the world.

Medieval philosophers divided human beings into four basic types: melancholic, choleric, sanguine and phlegmatic. Psychologists who study individual differences today employ rather similar notions about temperament. It is now believed that some babies are naturally timid and inhibited, while others tend to be over-active and inattentive. Some babies seem naturally easy, eager to embrace new experiences, while others remain slow to warm up, preferring the familiar to the new.

Such differences can show themselves early on, in particular when new experiences are introduced, such as the first bath, first solid food or first day at the play group or nursery school. Many believe that such differences remain stable throughout life. Thomas, Chess and Birch (1968) claim that 70 per cent of 'difficult' infants in their survey needed psychiatric treatment later in life compared with only 18 per cent of 'easy' infants.

How important is temperament in determining what sort of people we are?

Sex and gender

Aggression, hyperactivity, delinquency and anti-social behaviour occur more in males than females. This finding is repeated across studies in so many different cultures that some biological explanation seems appropriate. But cultural factors also play a large part. For instance, the ratio of male to female delinquents in Britain has decreased sharply in the last forty years (West, 1982). No one would suggest this difference has occurred because of changes in female biology; rather, it is cultural expectations about the nature of femininity that have changed. There are now more females pursuing traditionally male roles in school, jobs and sports. Crime is just another area where women are now more active. Campbell (1987) concludes that among female juvenile delinquents, an absence of emotional attachment to the mother is more predictive of criminal behaviour than is the type of control and discipline imposed by the father.

But while there are often severe pressures upon mothers in terms of marriage breakdown, work expectations and difficulties in arranging child care, many of the traditional pressures bearing upon all females also remain in place. At school, boys tend to do more than their fair share of talking in the classroom. In the media, emphasis on beauty and marriage rather than brains and careers persists where females are concerned. Many women with children do most of the child care, sometimes giving up or damaging their career prospects in the process.

So, differences between the sexes continue to have a significant impact on individual lives. Biologically, women tend to live longer than men and seem more resistant to disease. Culturally, pressure on both sexes to behave in certain traditional ways remains strong, although more people are now trying to break free from such stereotypes. For a full discussion of these and other issues arising from this topic, see also the companion unit *Sex, Gender and Identity* by Patricia J.Turner.

SAQ
11

Females now have the same advantages as males at school and in the workplace. True or false?

Intelligence

Both genetic and environmental factors are important in the growth of intelligence. But while intellectual parents are more likely to have intelligent children, it is impossible to measure the respective influences of genetic information and environmental stimulation upon individual **IQ**. Babies who quickly get bored with familiar objects but regain interest when shown a new stimulus tend to be those who are more intelligent at school. Much also depends on how much encouragement and stimulation they receive, particularly in the family environment between the ages of three and five. Adopted children brought up in privileged homes are, on average, 12 points ahead on the IQ scale compared with those brought up in disadvantaged homes (Rutter, 1985).

Each person's intelligence is therefore a combination of natural characteristics influenced by the environmental stimulation they have received. Such stimulation is particularly important during childhood, with appropriate levels often having a significant effect on the child's later self-esteem.

Low self-confidence and self-esteem may follow from a disadvantaged childhood. Yet some people who manage to overcome the challenges of their childhood seem to come out stronger through the knowledge of having defeated adversity. For example, older children who successfully took on a great deal of family responsibility during the pre-war economic slump often seem strengthened by this experience. In their survey of the children of Kauai island in Hawaii, Werner and Smith (1982) describe how these young people became more resilient through having to cope with stressful life events. The authors believe there is a 'self-righting' tendency within many of those born in disorganized, disturbed families, showing itself in the way that some such children still manage to make a success of their lives however unpromising a start they have had.

No psychologist fully understands why some children succumb to **learned helplessness** or deviancy following disadvantaged family conditions while others manage to turn adversity into personal strength. What is certain is that no individual can ever be completely written off: there will always be some who manage to overcome all obstacles.

SOMETHING TO TRY
Search through the 'biography' section of your nearest library for an account of someone who made good despite an impoverished childhood. What personality and environmental influences in their youth seem to you most important in accounting for their later success?

Cultural factors

Socio-economic background

Performance in school tends to be closely related to socio-economic background. Children from poor families living in inadequate housing often achieve less in their education, changing schools more often and attending lessons less frequently. More privileged children have a better chance of succeeding at school, of receiving good support at home and of attending schools with higher academic standards.

Clearly people from impoverished backgrounds with poor academic records usually find it harder to get better-paid jobs with good prospects. But again much depends on each individual and personal qualities such as a general determination to succeed.

Family

In extreme cases, an unsupportive family can make it hard for children to progress towards a contented and moderately prosperous life. The evidence from many studies shows that delinquent children often come from families where there is parental criminality, family tension, poor supervision and weak parent/child relationships.

Children can have sharply varying experiences within one family. Those who receive less affection and more criticism from their parents than other siblings tend to show more problem behaviour and develop low self-esteem. If an older child takes on a dominant role, such as leader, this may make it more likely that the next child becomes a typical follower. In other families, siblings may act together as one unit. These different family patterns may have an important bearing on children and upon what type of adult they become.

School and peer group

While no school can influence what children are like before they start their education, schools still have a considerable effect upon academic performance and standard of conduct. Children in Britain spend a minimum of 11 years at school, some 15 000 hours in all, and the quality of their education will usually have far-reaching effects on their lives.

In one survey of primary schools, pupils performed 19 per cent worse than average in the least good school and 28 per cent better than average in the best. Children who went to the least effective schools were twice as likely to show poor attendance, and these poor attenders were then twice as likely to leave school without passing any examinations. As adults, they were twice as likely to go into unskilled work and, in general, had poor employment records (Rutter *et al.* 1979). In the case of children already at risk, such as those brought up in institutional care, those who later become successful often report good experiences at school. One particularly concerned and caring teacher can have a positive upon such pupils, especially when this good influence is supported by the pupil's parents or guardians.

More is known about the negative than the positive effects of a particular group of friends upon an individual. Delinquency rates are higher for pupils in schools where there are many pupils who leave with poor or no academic qualifications. Moving a pupil away from an underprivileged school and its surroundings sometimes leads to a drop in delinquency, with a consequent improvement in that pupil's chances of becoming a non-delinquent adult (Rutter, 1979).

Parents often blame other adolescents for having a bad influence upon their own teenagers. But another point of view is that adolescents are responsible for their own choices, and that it is unfair to blame others for the difficulties they may sometimes get into. What do you think?

Interactions

Having looked at some significant biological factors and environmental factors, the next task is to assess the different ways in which these interact in individual lives.

Timing

This is important in all human affairs. The death of a parent is easier to accept when that parent is 80 rather than 30. Pregnancy is usually easier to deal with for a woman in her twenties within a stable relationship than it is for an unmarried mother at a younger age. It is not simply *what* happens that matters, but *when*.

The meaning of experience

Much depends upon the meaning each individual ascribes to their experience. A person who has always been more criticized than encouraged may become used to the idea of failure, while someone who has been praised and supported may approach life more positively. How individuals feel about themselves has a powerful effect on their own behaviour: what they expect from life and how others see them. But the expectations of others, in turn, affect each individual; children who are seen as 'naughty' or 'bad' often receive negative responses from others, even when they are not behaving badly. Girls who are encouraged to behave in traditionally feminine ways may soon take on such conduct as their own. Expectations can become self-fulfilling: once individuals have internalized strong social stereotypes, they may behave in ways that encourage others to accept such stereotyped behaviour as typical of what to expect from them (Jones, 1977).

The accentuation principle

People who already have serious problems are likely to be worse affected by other potentially difficult life-events such as unemployment, pregnancy, economic privation or an unhappy marriage. In times of particular stress, one extra difficulty sometimes accentuates an individual's problems to a point where they may no longer be able to cope. Yet the same difficulty may mean less if the individual concerned only has that particular problem to deal with.

For example, a survey found that adult criminality is associated with a combination of aggression, hyperactivity, inattention and poor peer relationships. But individuals who only show a high level of aggression have no particular tendency towards crime (Magnusson and Bergman, 1990).

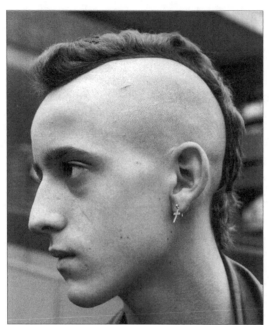

Historical and geographical factors

A peasant farmer in India is going to have a very different type of life from a merchant banker living in London. The lives we all lead are dependent upon the opportunities available to us as well as on our own ability to make the most of them. Within Britain or any other country, life for most is better when there is high employment and a stable economy. The cultural climate of the times is also important: young adults in the 1960s behaved differently from similar adults today.

Are our lives determined by our past experience?

An individual's passage through life is guided by a variety of different influences, but how these interact with each other is always hard to quantify.

Temperament and genetic inheritance are important predispositions in individual personality. Children who are bright and have easy personalities are more likely to receive positive reactions from others, including their parents. Difficult, inattentive and aggressive children more often have a negative effect upon their immediate environment at home and at school. Both types of child may change as they grow up, but a happy childhood is generally a good predictor of adult success. By contrast, aggression and poor social relationships at 13, together with inattention and hyperactivity, are strongly linked with later adult problems.

Early environmental conditions usually have an important and fundamental effect upon the individual. For example: early, appropriate stimulation can speed up the growth of language and intelligence, providing an educational advantage that may prove important in adulthood. Good parental example can lead to the lifelong internalization of positive values, standards and attitudes.

But other early negative experiences can predispose individuals towards aggression. These include: family disruption; poor family relationships; a history of family criminality and ineffective supervision and family discipline. Children from chronically disadvantaged families tend to start school with fewer learning skills and less effective parental support. They are also more likely to be involved in accidents at home or on the road; to experience acute stress, for example from bitter family arguments; to experience family breakdown or go into care (Wedge and Essen, 1982). As adults, such children are more likely to suffer from unemployment, marriage breakdown and trouble with the law. But this is not to say that a disadvantaged childhood necessarily leads to a troubled adulthood. Late adoption or intensive remedial therapy with extremely deprived children can produce significant changes for the better. Sadly, this sort of intervention is rare. Good schooling, a move to a better environment, a good marriage or a satisfying job can all help to change an individual's pattern of negative behaviour.

Both Britain and America have experimented with providing special pre-school education to disadvantaged children. While such interventions have not led to spectacular rises in intelligence of school attainment, most researchers are agreed that the children involved and their parents have benefited from these interventions. As Rutter (1985a) puts it: 'The long-term educational benefits stem not from what children are specifically taught but from effects on children's attitudes to learning, on their self-esteem, and on their task orientation.' Sylva (1994) in a review of different intervention programmes noted the existence of greater aspirations among pupils in their later school life, and the presence of more positive habits, traits and dispositions. Pupils also tended to initiate more contact with the teacher. Their social skills were often superior to those other disadvantaged children who had received no pre-school help.

It is incorrect to be fatalistic about human development. Some behaviours can change dramatically – witness the sudden decline in delinquent or anti-social activities that so often takes place in early adult life. Similarly, it is wrong to describe human development as a series of regular, psychological stages. Differences in background, ability, **self-concept** and the ways in which people react to important life events make all sweeping generalizations unreliable where each individual is concerned. It is these differences which make it impossible to predict with any certainty why some people succeed while others fail. There is also the matter of individual choice. Smoking, heavy drinking and unprotected sex are now known to be dangerous; some people will persist in these activities while others will not.

Rutter (1989) provides an overall map for understanding what he terms as the different pathways taken by individuals from birth to death. He believes that events in childhood can point individuals in certain directions, although past behaviour and experience are never going to be a total guide for what is going to happen in the future. External factors also play a large part in determining the particular chain of events occurring in any one life.

One example of different pathways in action quoted by Rutter describes what happened when some children in care in one particular institution were distributed to different schools in the area. Children placed in the best schools had much better educational experiences than did those who went to the poorer ones. Those children who had better experiences were then as adults three times more likely to show evidence of careful planning in their choice of careers and marriage partners. The more stable marriages they tended to make had in turn a positive effect upon their own parenting skills.

It can therefore be seen that children from similarly disadvantaged backgrounds took significantly different pathways through life according to the chances offered to them at the time. Such good fortune can then prove self-reinforcing, with others reacting positively to individuals who have come to feel more positive about themselves. It is not just what happens to individuals that matters; it is also how individuals react to what happens that can be crucial. But Rutter suggests that the positive links made early on in the chain of events in any one life can be very important in predicting a successful outcome later. The more negative an individual's early experience, the more negative the eventual results are likely to be.

Rutter agrees that genetic and biological factors, such as late maturation, also have an important part in determining individual growth and development. Good cognitive and social skills can help to make individual success, together with a sense of self-esteem and self-efficacy. The various useful habits and cognitive sets that go towards sound coping skills all help enhance self-confidence. But ultimately each individual finds their own path, influenced by chance factors such as the timing of certain events or happenings as well as by the sum of their past behaviour and experience.

Psychology can be used to point out the wide variations in human development, but it becomes a dogma if we believe that pressures from the past will necessarily dictate the present or the future. Enough is known about human development to predict that while one aspect of personality or behaviour may be likely to lead to another, no particular progression is ever certain and should never be seen to be so. Much abnormal development, for example the reasons why some individuals go on to suffer from alcoholism or obsessive gambling, is still very imperfectly understood. Psychology has a lot to offer the understanding of human beings; it also still has a lot to learn itself.

SOMETHING TO TRY

Read the following character description:

'John has just started a third term for burglary. Addicted to heroin, he has an illegitimate child from a relationship that soon ended. He has had no training since leaving school, and at 27 no record of steady employment. He has made one suicide attempt.'

What type of background is most likely to have produced a character like John? Write a short biography of him, guessing at the most important factors throughout his life that may have led him to his present predicament.

ASSIGNMENTS

Write one of the following essays to hand in to your tutor for marking. Spend no more than 45 minutes on the actual writing of the essay, although your planning and reading will take longer.

1. Adolescence is a time of unusual stress in the life of the individual. Write why you agree or disagree with this statement.

2. 'The child is father of the man'. But how much do childhood influences determine the type of adult we become?

FURTHER READING

RUTTER, M. and RUTTER, M. (1992) *Developing Minds: Challenge and Continuity across the Life Span*. London: Penguin.
COLEMAN, J. C. and HENDRY, L. (1990) *The Nature of Adolescence*. London: Routledge.

REFERENCES

ATTIE, I. and BROOKS-GUN, J. (1989) . Development of eating problems in adolescent girls; a longitudinal study. *Developmental Psychology*, 25, 70 – 79.

BAHR, S. J. and PETERSON, E. T. (Eds) (1989) *Aging in the family*. Lexington, Mass: D.C.Heath.

BELSKY, J. (1984) The determinants of Parenting: A Process. *Child Development*, 55. 83 – 96.

BENEDICT, R. (1934) *Patterns of Culture*. Boston: Houghton Mifflin.

BERNARD, J. (1982) *The Future of Marriage*. New Haven: Yale University Press.

CAMPBELL, A. (1987) Self-reported delinquency and home life. Evidence from a sample of British girls. *Journal of youth and adolescence*, 16, 167 – 177.

CATTELL, R. B. (1971) *Abilities: Their structure, growth and action*. Boston: Houghton Mifflin.

COLEMAN, J. C. and HENDRY, L. (1990) *The Nature of Adolescence*. London: Routledge.

CHERRY, N. (1984) Nervous strain, anxiety and symptoms amongst 32-year-old men at work in Britain. *Journal of Occupational Psychology*, 57, 95 – 105.

DANIEL, W. W. (1968) *Racial discrimination in England*. Harmondsworth: Penguin.

DICKENS, W. J. and PERLMAN, D. (1981) Friendship over the Life-cycle. IN DUCK, S. and GILMOUR, R. (Eds) *Personal Relationships* 2. London: Academic Press.

DWECK, C. S. and ELLIOT, E. S. (1988) An approach to motivation and achievement. *Journal of Personality and Social Psychology*, 54. (1) 5 – 12.

ELDER, G. H. (Ed) (1985) *Life Course Dynamics: Trajectories and Transitions 1968 – 1980*. Ithica: Cornell University Press.

ELKIND, D. (1981) *Children and Adolescents*. New York: Oxford University Press.

ERIKSON, E. (1968) *Identity, Youth and Crisis*. New York: Norton.

FURSTENBERG, F. F. , BROOKS-GUNN, S. and MORGAN, S. P. (1987) *Adolescent Mothers in Later Life*. Cambridge: Cambridge University Press.

HAYES, C. D. (Ed) (1987) *Risking the Future: Adolescent Sexuality, Pregnancy and Childbearing*, Vol.1. Washington, DC: National Academy Press.

HODGES, J. and TIZZARD, B. (1989) Social and family relationships of ex-institutional adolescents. *Journal of Child Psychology and Psychiatry*, 30, 77 – 97.

HYDE, J. and FENNEMA, E. (1990) Gender differences in maths performance: a meta-analysis. *Psychological Bulletin*, 107(2), 139 – 153.

JAHODA, M., LAZARSFELD P. F., and ZEISEL, H. (1971) *Marienthal: the sociology of an unemployed community*. Chicago: Aldine-Atherton.

JONES, R. A. (1977) *Self-fulfilling Prophecies; Social, Psychological and Physiological Effects of Expectancies*. Hillsdale, New Jersey: Lawrence Erlbaum.

KALISH, R. A. (1985) The social context of death and dying. In R. H. BINSTOCK and E. SHANAS (Eds) *Handbook of Aging and the Social Sciences*. New York: Van Nostrand Reinhold.

KRUSS, G. (1992) *Young People and Health*. Belfast: Whiterock.

KÜBLER-ROSS, E. (1969) *On Death and Dying*. New York: Macmillan.

LAMB, M. E. and BORNSTEIN, M. (Eds) (1984) *Developmental Psychology: An Advanced Textbook*. Hillsdale, New Jersey: Lawrence Erlbaum.

MAGNUSSON, D. and BERGMAN, L. R. (1990) A pattern approach to the study of pathways from childhood to adulthood. In ROBBINS, L. and RUTTER, M. (Ed) *Straight and deviant pathways from childhood to adulthood*. Cambridge: Cambridge University Press.

NEUGARTEN, B. L. and WEINSTEIN, K. K. (1964) The changing American grandparent. *Journal of Marriage and the Family*, 26, 199 – 204.

RABBITT, P. and GOWARD, L. (1994) Age, information processing speed and intelligence. *Quarterly Journal of Experimental Psychology*, 47A, 741 – 760.

ROLLINS, B. C. and FELDMAN, H. (1970) Marital satisfaction over the family life cycle. *Journal of Marriage and the Family*, 32, 20 – 28.

RUTTER, M. *et al*, (1976) Adolescent Turmoil; Fact or Fiction? *Journal of Child Psychology and Psychiatry*, 17, 35 – 56.

RUTTER, M. (1979) *Changing Youth in a Changing Society: Patterns of Adolescent Development and Disorder*. London: Nuffield Provincial Hospitals Trust.

RUTTER, M. (1985) Family and school influence on cognitive development. *Journal of Child Psychology and Psychiatry*, 26, 683 – 704.

RUTTER, M. (1985a) Family and school influences on behavioural development. *Journal of Child Psychology and Psychiatry*, 26, 349 – 68.

RUTTER, M. (1989) pathways from childhood to social life. *Journal of Child Psychology and Psychiatry*, 30, 23 – 51.

RUTTER, M., MAUGHAN, B., MORTIMORE, P., and OUSTON, J. (1979) *Fifteen Thousand Hours; Secondary Schools and their Effects on Children*. London: Open Books.

RUTTER, M. and RUTTER, M. (1992) *Developing Minds: Challenge and Continuity across the Life Span*. London: Penguin.

SCHAIE, K. W. and WILLIS, S. L. (1986) *Adult Development and Aging*. Boston: Little, Brown & Co.

SCHUMACHER, E. F. (1979) *Good Work*. New York: Harper Calophon Books.

SYLVA, K. (1994) School influences on childhood development. *Journal of Child Psychology and Psychiatry*, 35, 135 – 170.

THOMAS, A., CHESS, S., and BIRCH, H. (1968) *Temperament and Behavioural Disorders in Childhood*. New York: New York University Press.

WEDGE, P. and ESSEN, J. (1982) *Children in Adversity: The National Children's Bureau Report on Britain's Disadvantaged 11-16 Year-Olds*. London: Pan.

WELLINGS, K., FIELD, J., JOHNSON, A. M. and WANDSWORTH, J. (1994) *National Survey of Sexual Attitudes and Lifestyles*. London: Penguin.

WERNER, E. E. and SMITH, R. S. (1982) *Vulnerable but Invincible; A Longitudinal Study of Resilient Children and Youth*. New York: McGraw-Hill.

WEST, D. J. (1982) *Delinquency: Its Roots, Careers and Prospects* London: Heinemann.

ANSWERS TO SELF-ASSESSMENT QUESTIONS

SAQ 1 They all do. Psycholanalysis stresses the importance for the individual of early family environment, particularly where parents and other children are concerned. Sociologists stress the vital influence of society, peer groups and the world of work upon the individual. Cognitive psychologists stress the importance of the early stimulation gained from an infant's environment. Life span psychologists stress the way that external influences from the environment combine with the internal state of different individuals to make them the people they are.

SAQ 2 Puberty sometimes starts before adolescence, when a girl begins menstruating but otherwise remains a child in terms of her principal interests and attitudes. Adolescence can also start before puberty, with an older adolescent developing intellectually, psychologically and socially even though he or she remains in a pre-pubescent state.

SAQ 3 This depends. Anxiety can be caused by uneven physical growth, for example, an adolescent's nose may grow to full size before the rest of the face. There is also occasional worry about clumsiness, where adolescents unused to their larger limbs more often bump into objects or knock things over by mistake. Anxiety about appearing overweight also occurs, particularly with girls. On the other hand, boys usually welcome their new height and strength and girls may feel equally positive about their new womanly shapes. The odd facial spot or blackhead may prove a nuisance, but for most adolescents minor physical embarrassments like these are outweighed by the new confidence that comes once childhood is left behind and the rest of the world gradually starts taking them more seriously.

SAQ 4 1. Confusing the temporary with the lasting.

2. Believing others are as interested in what you do as you are yourself (imaginary audience).

3. Believing your own experience is quite unique, so separating yourself from any other adolescent who has ever lived (personal fable).

SAQ 5 An adolescent unable over time to acquire a stable sense of identity is seen by Erikson as suffering from a state of *identity diffusion*. In this state, he or she may persistently change their views and behaviour from one day to the next, bewildering others as well as themselves. He also thought it could be a mistake for an adolescent to foreclose all their personality options too soon, resulting in rigidity and excluding future possibilities of change. Some role-experimentation was a good idea, allowing individuals to try out different types of personality and behaviour for themselves. But serious and persistent identity diffusion, where individuals show no signs of coming together with age, is a different matter.

SAQ 6 This depends. Some adolescents and their parents can be at serious odds, particularly when there is a history of bad relationships extending back to childhood. Other parents who continue to treat their adolescents as children, still trying to dictate everything from style of haircuts to bedtimes, will usually provoke some hostile reactions. But parents able to adjust to a teenager's need for more independence, can get on well with their children. While there may be some disagreements about matters of taste, basic ideas about morality, politics and standards of personal behaviour are often quite similar between the generations.

SAQ 7 No. While there may be some initial excitement and interest in a relationship based on different personalities and attitudes, in the long term most people seem to fare better with those who share many of their chief interests and characteristics.

SAQ 8 Yes and no. Stealing and vandalism generally fall off anyway among most young adults who have a minor criminal past. Marriage to a law-abiding spouse certainly helps consolidate this process of greater respectability. For more hardened delinquent adults who continue to offend at the same rate as they did when younger, the picture is less clear. While there may be some improvements after marriage to a non-criminal spouse, minor delinquency may still occur on occasions.

SAQ 9 No. It all depends on what is happening to the individual at the time. Positive factors can include:

- Satisfaction at work.
- More money to spend once children have left.
- A fulfilling lifestyle.
- Continued good health and mental alertness.
- Enjoyment of the achievements of middle age, such as social status, a house, a stable marriage and fewer financial problems.

Negative factors can include:

- Dissatisfaction at work, redundancy or unemployment.
- Strain in the marriage, sometimes becoming more obvious once children have left.
- Poor physical and/or mental health.
- Worry about one's ageing parents.
- A sense of not having achieved enough, often coupled with a feeling that it is now too late to start afresh.

Whether positive factors outweigh negative ones or vice versa depends upon the individual concerned and their particular situation.

SAQ 10 None of these stereotypes need necessarily be true.

1. Mental powers diminish in some areas but people remain as intelligent as they always were, especially when individuals are still open to new ideas.

2. Hearing and eyesight weaken. But general health — building on a good foundation laid down earlier in life — can still remain good enough for an old person to continue working in less strenuous jobs should they wish to.

3. Only a small proportion of elderly people suffer from senility.

4. Sexual activity can last indefinitely, providing there is both health and the will.

SAQ 11 False. In co-educational schools, boys tend to talk more and to gain more of their teachers' attention. They are also often expected to work harder and more successfully at scientific and mathematical subjects. Within marriage, women still take responsibility for most of the child care, with consequent negative effects upon their career prospects. Prejudice against employing and promoting women in male-dominated professions is still quite common.